Reptile Keeper's Guides

AQUATIC TURTLES

Sliders, Cooters, Painted, and Map Turtles

R. D. Bartlett
Patricia Bartlett

With Photographs by the Authors

BARRON'S

Acknowledgments

As usual, we have many friends and colleagues to thank for their help with this book. Time and again Rob MacInnes, Bill Pierce, and Chuck Hurt of Glades Herp, Inc. provided us with photo opportunities. Don Hamper, Rick Van Dyke, Clive Longden, Dennis Uhrig, and Charlie Green offered stimulating thoughts on albino and pastel red-eared sliders and on Big Bend sliders. Kenny Wray and Scott Cushnir accompanied us on many field photography fact-finding trips. To all, and to all others with whom we have talked over the years, our sincere thanks.

And to our editor, Anna Damaskos, we say thanks again.

All inquiries should be addressed to:
Barron's Educational Series, Inc.
250 Wireless Boulevard
Hauppauge, NY 11788
http://www.barronseduc.com

Library of Congress Catalog Card No. 2002026264

International Standard Book No. 0-7641-2278-9

Library of Congress Cataloging-in-Publication Data
Bartlett, Richard D., 1938–
    Aquatic turtles : sliders, cooters, painted, and map turtles /
R. D. Bartlett, Patricia Bartlett.
      p. cm. — (Reptile keeper's guides)
      ISBN 0-7641-2278-9
    1. Turtles as pets. I. Bartlett, Patricia Pope, 1949–   II. Title.
SF459.T8 B3678   2003
639.3'92—dc21   2002026264

Printed in China
9 8 7 6 5 4 3

Contents

Introduction

Although turtle fanciers do not always know their proper names, they have been having a love affair with baby sliders, cooters, painted turtles, and map turtles for more than sixty years. Collectively, these are the baby "green turtles, yellow-bellies, gray-backs," and "stripe-necks" that were once found on the pet counters of almost every five-and-ten-cent store in America, and in similar outlets elsewhere in the world. Housed in flat turtle bowls with dyed oyster-shell chips and an inch of dirty water, the little turtles sold for 29 to 59 cents. If you wanted one with a gaudily enameled shell (often decorated further with decals of the flag, a flower, or a palm tree), you might have to part with 89 cents. In the early days you simply brought the little turtle home (usually with a can of dried ant eggs—an absolutely useless food) for its diet and found a little bowl to put it in. In the 1950s plastic turtle bowls, often with a rather hideous plastic palm tree as a removable fixture, came into vogue. Only the manufacturers know how many tens of thousands of these unsuitable turtle homes have been sold over the decades, but believe it or not, they are still available today!

The accepted common names of these turtles are unquestionably fanciful. They are known as sliders (genus *Trachemys*), cooters (genus *Pseudemys*), painted turtles (genus *Chrysemys*), and map turtles (genus *Graptemys*). The first three of these groups are closely allied; the last, consisting of the map turtles, is more distant.

The types most commonly seen in the five-and-dimes of yesteryear and the pet trade of today are of North American origin. In fact, of the four genera, only the slider works its way significantly farther southward than the border rivers along Texas's Rio Grande (or, if you prefer, Mexico's Rio Bravo).

Note the characteristic vertical light marks on the shell of this adult common red-eared slider.

Aquatic Turtles as Pets

Today, even as in Victorian times, baby aquatic turtles are commonly kept as pets. Providing you can give them the conditions they need, they make fine pets indeed. A few points should be foremost in your thoughts when you are considering a baby aquatic turtle. First, the turtles are babies, and that means that, if given proper care, they will grow. Second, the purchase of a turtle should be viewed as a long-term commitment. Red-eared sliders *(Trachemys scripta elegans)* have been known to live for more than fifty years in captivity! And, third, a turtle bowl is not an adequate home for a baby turtle.

How big will these turtles grow? In many cases, bigger than a dinner plate. The sliders attain a shell length of 8 to 12 inches (20–30 cm), some cooters may exceed 15 inches (38 cm) in length, and varying by race, the painted turtles reach 4.5 to 9.5 inches (11.2–24 cm) when adult. The size of the map turtles is variable by species and by sex. The males of most map turtles are adult at between 3.5 and 5.5 inches (9–14 cm) in shell-length. The female map turtles are often

more than twice the length of the males of the same species. No wonder a turtle bowl is inadequate!

What conditions do these baby turtles need to keep them responsive and healthy in captivity? Actually the conditions don't change much throughout a turtle's long life. It is the size of the facilities needed to provide those conditions that must be altered. Although a baby red-eared slider may thrive in a 5-gallon tank, an adult will require a tank of no less than 40 gallons capacity.

The aquatic turtles we are discussing here are referred to collectively as basking turtles. After overnighting or swimming in the water, these turtles bask in the warming rays of the sun to elevate their body temperature. All of these turtles are inveterate

Rick Van Dyke specializes in breeding many kinds and colors of sliders. Pictured is a large adult pastel common red-eared slider.

Despite having bright eyes, albino turtles often have impaired vision. This is a common red-eared slider.

The Ouachita map turtle has a broad yellow marking behind the eye and large yellow spots along its jaws.

baskers, sitting, sometimes for hours, on exposed sunny snags and banks. In this way they elevate their body temperature to its optimum level, diving into the water to cool off if they get too hot. Preferred basking haulouts are smooth, exposed snags, smooth rocks sloping upward from the water, or even muddy banks. To prevent shell disorders, captive turtles should be provided the same kind of haulouts. We use smooth, weathered driftwood and provide enough surface for the turtle(s) to easily balance, move a little, and dry completely. Textured plastic and other haulouts are commercially available. These are more easily sterilized than driftwood. In outside ponds a bark covered limb (do not use cedar or other aromatic wood) may be used and replaced when necessary.

The daytime temperature at the summit of our haulouts in our indoor tanks varies from 95° to 102°F (35–39°C). This is provided by UV-A heat-lamp bulbs that are turned on during daylight hours. The high temperature of the haulout in the outside pool is much more variable, being cooler, or even warmer, depending on the season and whether or not the sun is shining. The water temperature varies from about 65°F (18°C) (outside pond on a cool winter day) to 85°F (29°C) (indoor tank in midsummer).

To thrive, to *really* thrive, these pretty and interesting turtles need space to swim and bask in ample, clean quarters having both a suitable water and basking-station temperature. Brilliant (preferably full-spectrum) illumination, and a healthful diet are also needed.

One, two, or even four baby turtles can be housed temporarily in a properly appointed 10- or 15-gallon aquarium.

The same number of 4-inch-long specimens will require nothing less than a 30-, and preferably a 40-gallon aquarium, and one or two adult turtles will need a 75-gallon or larger tank. When indoors, ours are kept in filtered aquaria of 150- and 220-gallon size. During the late spring, summer, and early autumn months, the turtles are housed outdoors in a sunken 270-gallon preformed, filtered, vinyl garden pond.

However you choose to house your aquatic turtles, it is imperative that you provide all of the above criteria.

Besides being filtered (indoors we use submersible power-head pumps on large sponge filters, which are cleaned at least once weekly; outside we use a pond filter), the water in your turtle tank will require periodic changing. If you accomplish this by means of a siphon tube, do not start the siphon by sucking on it. To do so is to ask for gastrointestinal problems. The more turtles you have and the larger they are, the more often the water will require changing. This holds true in a garden pond as well as in an indoor aquarium. A self-priming pond pump is an ideal way to remove the water from either indoor or outdoor units. The aquarium water may also be removed by connecting plastic tubing of proper diameter to the outflow of a running power head.

This alert common red-eared slider is swimming through the shallows of a small pond.

Handling Your Aquatic Turtle

Both before and after handling your baby turtle, always wash your hands carefully.

Although most aquatic turtles are hardy and easy to handle, they are better considered "look at and enjoy" rather than "pick-up-and-pet" pets.

Turtles can be handled, and some even become used to it, but many will

Salmonella and the Availability of Baby Turtles

Although baby turtles have been a mainstay of the pet industry for more than sixty years and continue to be readily available today through many venues, the sale of those with a shell length of less than 4 inches to casual hobbyists is technically illegal. A United States Public Health Service regulation enacted several decades ago restricts the sale of turtles or tortoises of less than 4 inches in shell length for anything other than research or scientific purposes. This regulation was formulated and passed in response to a salmonella scare. The rationale was that a toddler could unwittingly put a baby turtle in his or her mouth, thereby contracting salmonellosis. The 4-inch-criterion law was based not on being salmonella-free, but rather on being too big to be put into one's mouth. This of course ignores the fingers, unwashed after handling a turtle, that are put, still unwittingly, into a mouth.

Salmonella is an omnipresent bacterium. If a baby aquatic turtle is housed in unsanitary conditions, you can be just about certain that salmonella will be present in its quarters. The true solution is not one of turtle size, but rather a simple matter of cleanliness, and especially the washing of one's hands with an antibacterial soap after handling a baby turtle. In fact, carefully washing your hands both before and after handling a turtle, as well as any surfaces with which your turtle tank has come in contact, will do much more toward preventing an unpleasant bout with salmonella-induced gastrointestinal problems than worrying about the length of a turtle's shell.

nip (or bite hard!) if they feel insecure or threatened.

Do not place your turtle unheld on the open palm of an elevated hand. The little reptile can move with a surprisingly fast burst of speed, and if dropped, may break its shell or a limb.

Hold your turtle securely with fingers on each side of its shell or, if the specimen is large, with both hands. Keep your fingers away from the turtle's mouth. The neck is long, and a turtle can reach a considerable distance if it chooses to try to bite. If you are bitten, don't drop the turtle. If it doesn't release its grip right away, submerge your hand and the turtle in cool (not hot or cold) water. This will usually induce the turtle to release you almost immediately.

It is normal for a turtle to void the contents of its bladder and cloaca if frightened. When picked up, they often do so. Wash your hands (or other areas of your body) carefully if the turtle voids on you.

Dark pigment (melanin) has all but obscured the pattern and colors of this adult male common red-eared slider.

Gentle handling is the keynote to gaining the confidence of your pet aquatic turtle. Remember that the shell is a living, growing, and feeling part of your turtle. To ascertain this you need usually only touch the rear of the shell while watching the movements of the

turtle's anterior. A touched turtle may withdraw appendages into its shell, spasmodically move its legs, or open its mouth. Handle it gently and sparingly.

If you are able to refrain from constantly handling your aquatic turtles, and can provide them with the conditions they need, virtually all make fine pets. All of those discussed in these pages—the sliders, cooters, painted turtles, and map turtles—are captive-bred by the thousands annually and are readily available at various outlets. Many of the more uncommonly seen related species (see Other Species charts on pages 10, 12, and 14) are periodically offered by specialty dealers.

With that said, let's meet some of the better aquatic turtle pets.

The bright coloration of the plastron is retained throughout life by the western painted turtle.

Shades of green, red, and yellow make the western painted turtle one of the most beautiful North American turtles.

Species, Subspecies, and Color Morphs

The Yellow-Bellied Slider and Relatives

In one or another of its thirteen subspecies, the yellow-bellied slider, *(Trachemys scripta)* ranges southward from the northern United States, through Mexico and Central America, to northern South America. Although almost all of its races are seen occasionally in the pet trade, five types dominate. These are the yellow-bellied slider itself, the far better-known red-eared slider, *Trachemys scripta elegans*, and three Latin American races of red-ears, the ornate red-eared slider, *T. s. ornata*, the southern red-ear, *T. s. callirostris*, and the northern Venezuelan red-ear, *T. s. chichiriviche*.

Before moving onward, let's take a look at these five subspecies, beginning with the meaning of the name "slider." Strange though it may sound, the name was coined to describe the ease and agility with which a member of the species slides from its basking site into the safety of the water. Should you ever have an opportunity to watch one of these turtles in the wild or in a garden pool, you will see how appropriate the name is.

Hatchlings of the yellow-bellied slider *(Trachemys scripta scripta)* dull significantly in color within only a few months of hatching. The 1.25-inch-long hatchlings are almost round when viewed from above. The carapace of a yellow-bellied slider hatchling is of a green hue that blends well with the aquatic plants of its habitat. Each carapacial scute (scale) bears symmetrically arranged, thin, dark lines, and a broad vertical light bar in the center of each scute. The plastron (bottom shell) is yellow with a small, irregular, greenish spot on each anterior scute (sometimes on all scutes but the markings are most apparent anteriorly). The head tail and limbs are primarily green, but a

A yellow-bellied slider surfaces for a breath.

vivid yellow, vertically oriented cheek patch is typical.

Females tend to retain their juvenile color longer than males, but the shells of adults of both sexes are often almost black. The eyes are green. All feet are webbed, the rear feet fully so.

This subspecies is native to the southeastern United States. At the periphery of its range it often interbreeds with the red-eared slider.

Native to the Mississippi River valley, the red-eared slider is a hardy turtle that is surprisingly temperature tolerant. Because it has long been one of the world's most popular reptile pets, unwanted, released red-eared sliders are now found in many areas of the United States where they are not native. They are also established in New Zealand, Australia, France, Germany, Mexico, Venezuela, Japan, and elsewhere.

Baby basking turtles of all kinds (like this ornate red-eared slider) find seclusion amidst aquatic vegetation.

The babies of the red-eared slider are beautiful and active little turtles. At hatching their carapace is a bright green with vertical yellowish marking on each carapacial scute. The brilliance of the babies quickly fades. By the time the turtles are 3 or 4 inches (8–10 cm) in length, the green has faded to olive, and it may fade even more quickly from that age onward. This is especially true of males, which may become so suffused with melanin that they

The northern Venezuelan red-eared slider is a beautiful creature.

Beautiful as a baby, the southern red-eared slider becomes very dark as an adult.

The Other Red-Ears and the Big Bend Slider

- Rio Guaiba slider, *T. dorbigni brasiliensis*, Rio Guaiba drainage of Brazil
- Southern slider, *T. d. dorbigni*, Argentina, Uruguay, and possibly adjacent Brazil
- Big Bend slider, *T. gaigeae*, the Big Bend region of Texas, southeastern New Mexico, and adjacent Mexico
- Gulf coastal plain slider, *T. scripta cataspila*, Gulf coastal plain of Mexico south to Vera Cruz
- Yellow-eared slider, *T. s. grayi*, Pacific coastal plain of Mexico, from Oaxaca to northern Guatemala
- Rio Fuerte Slider, *T. s. hiltoni*, Sonora and Sinaloa, Mexico
- Baja slider, *T. s. nebulosa*, Mexico's southern Baja peninsula
- Cuatro Cienegas Slider, *T. s. taylori*, Coahuila, Mexico
- Cumberland slider, *T. s. troosti*, Cumberland Plateau region of southwestern Virginia and northeastern Tennessee
- Vera Cruz slider, *T. s. venusta*, Mexico's Atlantic and Gulf drainages from Vera Cruz to Quintana Roo.
- Yaqui slider, *T. s. yaquia,* Sonora, Mexico

turn nearly, or entirely, black. The plastrons of hatchlings have rather intricate circular or elongate markings on all scutes. These, too, fade with growth and advancing age.

One or more strains of red-eyed albino red-eared sliders have been developed and are now commonly available. Like many albino animals, the albino sliders often have impaired vision, and although olfactory cues will tell them that food is available, the turtles may have difficulty finding it. Once the scent has alerted the turtles to the presence of food, the turtles just swim about until they bump into pieces that are then grasped and swallowed. Albino red-ear babies are white with pink facial markings and yellowish highlights on the carapace. Adults are more yellowish overall and have coral-red cheeks.

"Pastel" red-ears are also available in the pet trade. Because these turtles often have malformed shell scutes and/or truncated snouts as well as strange colors, it seems probable that most are the result (at least in part) of nonoptimal incubation temperatures. Pastel red-ears have shells interestingly colored in tans, strange greens, and near turquoise, and often have greater amounts of red on the face than normal. It will be interesting to see whether any of these prettily colored variations become genetically stablized.

Both the yellow-bellied and the red-eared slider are moderate-size races. Both attain a carapace length of 11 inches (28 cm), but specimens having a shell length of 8 to 10 inches (20–25 cm) are far more common. Unfortunately, even turtles this shell length become a real chore to maintain indoors.

The three most commonly encountered Latin American forms are the ornate red-eared slider, the southern red-eared slider, and the northern Venezuelan red-eared slider.

The ornate red-ear is native to the Pacific drainages of Mexico, and from there ranges southward through Central America to northern Colombia. The yellow or red ear patch extends forward all the way to the orbit. One of the larger races, this turtle attains a carapace length of 15 inches (38 cm).

The southern red-ear occurs in the Caribbean drainages of Colombia and Venezuela. Its ear marking, which is red in color, does not usually reach the eye. Both of these races have large, dark, plastral figures. This pretty turtle attains 10 inches (25 cm) in length.

The northern Venezuelan red-eared slider is a beautiful race with a

A prettily marked Florida red-bellied cooter.

broad, teardrop-shape, deep red ear marking. This marking is broadest posteriorly and starts well posterior to the orbit. Like many of the tropical races of the red-ear, this form, too, has a dark plastral figure. The maximum size for this race is 13 inches (32.5 cm).

The Cooters

The big turtles of the genus *Pseudemys* are closely related to the sliders, and in some areas representatives of the two genera can be seen together. Their common name was derived from the African word, in several dialects "kuta," which means turtle. Of the approximately eight species (taxonomic designations are unsettled at the moment), only two are pet trade staples. These are the common river cooter, *P. concinna concinna*, and the Florida red-bellied cooter, *P. nelsoni*. Most are common turtles, but one, the Alabama red-bellied cooter, is on the federal endangered species list and cannot be collected or used for commercial purposes without a permit.

Like the red-ears and yellow-bellies, these turtles are all quite pretty

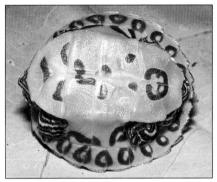

The plastral color of Florida red-bellied cooters actually varies from the orange—red displayed by this hatchling to a brighter red or a pure yellow.

Other Cooters

- Alabama red-bellied cooter, *Pseudemys alabamensis,* Alabama's Mobile Bay
- Suwannee cooter, *Pseudemys concinna suwanniensis,* northwestern Florida
- Coastal plain cooter, *Pseudemys floridana,* Atlantic and gulf coastal plains from extreme southeastern Virginia to northern Florida and eastern Alabama.
- Rio Grande cooter, *Pseudemys gorzugi,* the Rio Grande from southern Texas to central New Mexico
- Peninsula cooter, *Pseudemys peninsularis,* peninsula Florida
- Northern red-bellied cooter, *Pseudemys rubriventris,* southeastern Massachusetts to northeastern Virgina. Spotty distribution.
- Texas river cooter, *Pseudemys texana,* much of central Texas

and contrastingly colored in greens and yellows when hatchlings, but they, too, dull in color with age. These are large turtles. The adult size of some can exceed a 16-inch (40-cm) carapace length. Adults are primarily herbivorous, but babies are very omnivorous.

The head pattern of the river cooter is strongly striate, lacking spots and vertical bars entirely. The carapace usually (but not invariably) bears a rearward-directed letter C and several oblong ocelli in the second costal scute (the lower row of large carapacial scales). All species are of southeastern distribution.

The Florida red-bellied cooter is one of the prettiest of the basking turtles. Although it darkens with age, it often retains at least some of its color and pattern, and some develop broad vertical bars of bright orange on their carapace. The babies are very brightly colored, often having a bright reddish-orange (but sometimes yellow) plastron. When viewed from above, the head will be seen to bear an arrow-shape marking, the shaft between the eyes and the point along the edges of the snout. Adults of this Floridian species can attain a carapace length of 14.5 inches (36 cm).

The Painted Turtles

The single species (four races) of painted turtle is assigned to the genus *Chrysemys.* Of the four subspecies, only two, the western (*C. picta bellii*) and the southern (*C. p. dorsalis*) are pet trade mainstays. The other two, the eastern painted turtle, *C. p. picta,* and the midland painted turtle, *C. p. marginata,* are occasionally locally available, but seldom on a wide-scale basis.

The orange vertebral stripe is a diagnostic marking of the southern painted turtle.

The identifying marks of this southern painted turtle are obscured by a veneer of duckweed.

The western painted turtle occurs in disjunct populations eastward from the Pacific Northwest to southwestern Ontario and southern Missouri. The largest and most colorful of the four races, this turtle tops out at 10 inches (25 cm) in shell length, but is usually smaller. The carapace is greenish with a network of light lines. The plastron is red with a large and variable central figure that follows the scute seams. The head, neck, and limbs are greenish striped with yellow.

The southern painted turtle is less colorful (but still very pretty), having a dark brown carapace with an orange vertebral stripe, a yellow belly, and a multi-striped yellow and brown head, neck, and legs. This subspecies is found from western Louisiana and extreme southeastern Oklahoma to Tennessee. The other two races intergrade widely and occur over much of the eastern United States north of central Georgia.

Painted turtles haul out to bask on snags, rocks, and the banks of the ponds and slow-moving rivers in which they live. They are more carnivorous throughout their lives than the related sliders and cooters, eating invertebrates, tadpoles, minnows, carrion, and some aquatic vegetation.

The Map Turtles

Only two of the thirteen described species of map turtles (genus *Graptemys*) are frequently seen in the pet trade. An additional one or two species are occasionally seen. There is marked sexual dimorphism in the turtles in this genus, with the adult male often being only 40–60 percent of the length of the adult female.

Note the brilliant yellow postorbital crescents on this baby Mississippi map turtle.

Other Species of Map Turtles

- Barbour's map turtle, *Graptemys barbouri*, Apalachicola and Chipola river systems of Florida's panhandle and adjacent Alabama
- Cagle's map turtle, *Graptemys caglei*, San Antonio and Guadalupe river systems of central Texas
- Escambia map turtle, *Graptemys ernsti*, Escambia River system of western Florida and adjacent Alabama
- Yellow-blotched map turtle (sawback), *Graptemys flavomaculata*, Mississippi's Pascagoula River system
- Northern map turtle, *Graptemys geographica*, much of central and eastern United States
- Pascagoula map turtle, *Graptemys gibbonsi*, Pascagoula to the Pearl River systems of Mississippi
- Delta map turtle (sawback), *Graptemys nigrinoda delticola*, Mobile and Tensaw rivers, southeastern Alabama
- Black-knobbed map turtle (sawback), *Graptemys nigrinoda nigrinoda*, Black Warrior River system, Alabama
- Ringed map turtle (sawback), *Graptemys oculifera*, Mississippi's Pearl River system, including adjacent Louisiana
- Alabama map turtle, *Graptemys pulchra*, Mobile Bay drainages throughout much of northern, central, and southern Alabama; northwestern and central western Georgia
- Texas map turtle, *Graptemys versa*, Colorado River system of central Texas

The species in this genus are often referred to in one of six ways: large species, small species, narrow-headed species, broad-headed species, map turtles, or sawbacks. The name "map turtle" is derived from the tracery of light lines present on upper shells of most species. "Sawback" refers to the high vertebral keels (knobs) borne by some species. As mentioned on page 13, the females are the largest. Those of some species may attain a carapace length of about 10 inches (25 cm).

Likewise, it is only the females of the broad-headed forms that actually develop an enlarged head. Those with enlarged heads feed upon molluscs and crustaceans; those with narrow heads (including the males and the subadult females of the broad-headed species) feed largely on the much tenderer fare of aquatic insects.

Among the map turtles are some that are common and have immense ranges, and others that are restricted to parts of a single river system and are rare to endangered in status.

A baby Sabine map turtle takes a swim.

A hatchling Sabine map turtle.

Inveterate baskers all, most of the map turtles are associated with river system habitats, including the associated oxbow lakes and backwaters, where they sun on exposed snags. These are among the wariest of turtles and very difficult to approach.

The two species (four subspecies) in the pet trade are both large forms. They are the two races of the false map turtle and the two races of the Ouachita map turtle. These (and all other map turtles) have gray or brownish-gray carapaces, yellowish to white plastrons (with variable dark markings), and gray heads and limbs that are variably patterned with yellow or orange.

The range of the false map turtle, *Graptemys pseudographica pseudographica*, follows the drainages of the Mississippi, Missouri, and Wabash rivers from the latitude of central Missouri northward to southcentral North Dakota, southeastern Minnesota, and central western Indiana. It hybridizes readily with both the Mississippi map turtle and the Ouachita map turtle where the ranges abut. The false map turtle has

a conspicuous, rounded or oval yellow spot behind the eye, but the lower neck stripes reach the eye. The false map has well-defined, dark projections from the rear of each vertebral scute. This means the scales along the midback have a pointed projection at the rear of each.

Rather than a spot, the facial pattern of the Mississippi map turtle, *G. p. kohni*, is dominated by a yellow to orange postorbital crescent that prevents the neck stripes from reaching the eye. Otherwise very similar to the more northerly false map turtle, the Mississippi map turtle ranges southward in the Mississippi Valley from central Illinois to the gulf coast.

The yellowish postorbital marking of the Ouachita (pronounced wah-chi-taw) map turtle, *G. o. ouachitensis*, is in the form of a square or rectangle. That of the more westerly Sabine map turtle, *G. o. sabinensis*, has softened

This is a common red-eared slider. Note that this example has only a single red postocular stripe.

The colors of this subadult pastel common red-eared slider have remained brilliant.

corners, and the postorbital marking takes on the shape of a circle or ellipse. The Ouachita map turtle also has a light spot on the upper jaw, below the eye. This is sometimes connected to other facial markings and may look like a moustache. An elongated light spot is present on the lower mandible. When all markings are large and well defined, they impart to the Ouachita map turtle a greasepainted, clownlike countenance. The subocular and mandibular spots (those beneath the eye and on the jawlines) of the Sabine map turtle are usually much reduced.

The Ouachita map turtle takes its name from one of the river systems in which it is common. It ranges northward up the Mississippi River valley to eastern Indiana along the Ohio River, and from there westward to southeastern Kansas and central Oklahoma. The Sabine map turtle is restricted to the drainage of the Sabine River system in western Louisiana and eastern Texas.

Turtle Farming

Although some of the baby turtles in today's pet trade may be collected from the wild, the vast majority of the hundreds of thousands sold annually are produced on turtle farms in Mississippi and Louisiana.

Traditionally, the red-eared slider has been bred in the greatest numbers. When I first visited a turtle farm in the 1960s, I was astounded at the complexity and scope of the operation. The farm was Delta Turtle Farm, owned by John Haga, a pioneer in the business. Haga was justifiably proud of his knowledge of the reproductive biology of the red-eared slider, as well as the size and the cleanliness of his operation. He was among the first to realize that improper husbandry led to a proliferation of salmonella and other pathogens, and feared that unless these organisms could be controlled, turtle farmers would be legislated out of business. While smaller turtle farmers were still feeding their animals nutria carcasses, Haga was helping to formulate and use a prepared turtle chow in his ponds. His thousands of breeders were bright-eyed, healthy, and multi-clutched each season. The eggs were removed from the nests, artificially incubated, and the myriad babies produced placed in the pet trade. During one of my visits Haga showed me a few interestingly colored baby red-ears that had hatched from a clutch that had inadvertently (and temporarily) been subjected to improper incubation temperatures. The hatchling turtles had tan to bluish-green carapaces with abnormal scutellation and strangely blotched red patterns on their heads (today these are purposely produced and marketed as pastels). On another of my visits Haga presented me with a remarkable pure white (leucistic) red-ear with jet black eyes, and a red-eyed albino. There was also an odd-looking, pale-colored Mississippi map turtle. This was long

before the selective breeding by hobbyists for designer colors, and the turtles were then simply considered unmarketable aberrancies.

Turtle farms still thrive today. The breeding of these little animals has become far more sophisticated. Baby red-eared sliders still dominate the trade, but Florida red-bellied cooters, common river cooters, snapping turtles, spiny soft-shelled turtles, and false map turtles are also produced in vast numbers. Most are exported, but interestingly, today, rather than being considered an unmarketable liability, both albino and pastel turtles are coveted and bring premium prices. How attitudes have changed.

How and Where to Buy Aquatic Turtles

The acquisition of an aquatic turtle (of any potential pet, for that matter) should be carefully considered before the actual acquisition. Be certain that you are able to devote the space and

When babies, common red-eared sliders usually have discrete markings on each plastral scute.

As they become older, a suffusion of dark pigment often obscures most or all markings on common red-eared sliders.

Despite having "pastel" coloration, the carapacial scutes of this baby common red-eared slider have developed normally.

Besides odd colors, common red-eared sliders occasionally have other genetic aberrancies—such as the two heads shown here. Despite this, the turtle functions well.

time needed (we urge you to consider the size that your turtle will eventually attain, not just the size of the hatchling) to adequately house and care for the baby as it grows. Although most aquatic turtles will quickly become tame and responsive captives, this does not mean that they will be easy to handle. If it becomes impossible for you to keep your aquatic turtle, it should be given to another hobbyist or, if of an uncommon species, to a zoological garden. It should not be released into the wild. Animals so released can only rarely find enough food to survive and, if they crossbreed with others of their species, alter the local gene pools. Finally, we urge you to familiarize yourself with all existing state and federal laws. Many turtles are now protected by law, and further regulations

pertaining to the sale and keeping of other species are pending. As a caring hobbyist, it is your responsibility not only to fully understand the needs of your turtle, but to know the legalities relating to collecting, sale, and transportation of these reptiles as well.

Subadult sliders, cooters, painted turtles, and map turtles of normal coloration are still readily available in many pet stores across the nation. Normally colored hatchlings are also still offered by many pet stores and reptile dealers. If purchasing a hatchling aquatic turtle in the United States, you will have to sign a release form indicating that those you buy with a shell length of less than 4 inches (10 cm) are for scientific or research purposes rather than pets. Any specimen of 4 inch or greater length can be legally purchased without documentation.

Buy your turtle only if it has been kept in clean facilities, does not have swollen (puffy) eyelids, and has a reasonably rigid shell. Baby turtles normally have a certain degree of pliability to the edges of the shell. This will become more solid with growth. We suggest that before purchase you watch the turtle in which you are interested feed. If you purchase your turtle sight unseen, such as by mail order, make

Common red-eared sliders of four-color morphs bask in the sunshine.

sure that the seller is reputable and assures you the turtle has fed. This is especially important with albino and pastel specimens, since the former often have problems with visual acuity and the latter are the result of incubation-temperature manipulation.

Albino and pastel phases of the red-eared slider (and sometimes other species) can be found offered for sale by breeders on the World Wide Web, at reptile expos, in the classified sections of reptile magazines, or at specialty reptile shops.

If you are not prone to making impulse purchases, reptile expos, now held in many larger cities in the United States, are enjoyable and often offer a great diversity of reptile life. Information about expos may be found on the Web and in the classified sections of reptile magazines.

Normally colored sliders, cooters, painted turtles, and the commonly offered map turtles sell for $10 to $20 each.

Hatchling albino red-eared sliders cost $100 to $300 each. Albinos of larger sizes and other species may cost significantly more.

Pastel red ears (pastel yellow-bellied sliders and Florida red-bellied cooters are also occasionally offered) vary in price according to the intricacy of the color aberrancy. Expect to pay $25 to $100 each.

Caging

Housing Your Aquatic Turtles

What we've been referring to as "aquatic turtles" are really semi-aquatic turtles. Although they forage under water, court and mate underwater, and hibernate underwater, all are air-breathing reptiles that leave the water to bask, to nest, and occasionally to search for habitat. It is to the water that they try to scramble when evading an enemy. Even the most aquatic of turtles, the various sea turtles, and the freshwater mata-mata and pig-nosed turtles breathe air and nest terrestrially.

Whether kept indoors in aquaria or outside in a garden pool, these turtles must be provided with clean, fresh swimming water, illuminated and warmed above water basking sites, and, if you hope to breed them, nesting sites.

What Is "Basking"?

Since turtles are ectothermic (the old term is "cold-blooded") they must regulate their body temperature through the use of external stimuli. The warmth of the sun is one such stimulus. To avail themselves of the sun's warming rays many turtles bask, but not all do so in a similar manner.

Basking allows turtles to thermoregulate—to regulate their body temperature—to reach the internal body temperature that is most optimal for each species. Some species, such as mud turtles, may merely seek the comparative warmth of shallow, quiet, water to elevate their body temperature. Others such as the common snapper float at the surface of the water—deep or shallow—on sunny days, allowing their dark color and body bulk to absorb and store the warmth. But the sliders, cooters, painted turtles, and map turtles actually leave the water to bask. These species are so physiologically and psychologically adapted for basking that they are referred to as "basking turtles." But even when basking, they are amazingly alert, and seldom are more than a footstep or two away from the watery medium in which they are most at home. Sliders, cooters, painted turtles, and map turtles use haulouts such as smooth banks, smooth emergent rocks, fallen trees overhanging the water, or other sun-bathed obstacles on which to bask and dry.

At optimal body temperature (often many degrees above the temperature of the waters in which they swim) bodily processes—circulation, feeding and digestion, reproductive urges, and escape mechanisms—are at

When basking quietly, many turtles, like the pictured albino common red-eared slider, extend their limbs fully and spread their toes wide.

This is the normal "wild color" of the common red-eared slider.

their peak. As the sun dries the turtle while it basks, ectoparasites, such as leeches, tend to drop off and potentially pathogenic bacteria are killed.

So, to say that a turtle basks merely means that in some way the creature avails itself of the warming rays of the sun to elevate body temperature.

A complacently basking slider or map turtle is often the very picture of contentment. The sunning turtle extends its neck to the fullest, sticks its back feet straight backward and separates the toes to expose as much of the interdigital webbing as possible. Although the forefeet are also extended, the claws are often fully in contact with the basking surface, ready to propel the turtle into a fast getaway if necessary.

When the turtle warms sufficiently, or is in danger of overheating, it may drop into the water to cool and forage. This alternating procedure may take place several times daily.

All of these turtles are strong swimmers, but one group in particular, the map turtles, are masters of this element. They are fast, agile, and so alert that it is difficult to understand how any ever wind up in the

pet trade. Sliders, cooters, painted turtles, and map turtles feed while submerged. Food is found by sight, by scent, and perhaps, by touch.

Aquatic Turtles Indoors

As we have already said, baby aquatic turtles will live well indoors, providing their needs are met. We usually have a few baby turtles housed in aquaria around the house. Two of our favorite setups are a 250-gallon aquarium with some large, hardy tropical fish and a number of map turtles, and a 150-gallon aquarium containing South American lungfish, angelfish, and a few sliders. Both aquaria are landscaped with a substrate of pea-size river rock, driftwood snags (some project above the water for basking platforms) Java moss, and Amazon swordplants. The tanks are filled to the top with water,

This pretty turtle is a naturally occuring intergrade between the yellow-bellied slider and the common red-eared slider.

Inveterate baskers, these captive black-knobbed map turtles are sunning on a floating piece of wood in an 8-foot-diameter stock-watering tank.

strongly illuminated with UV-A/UV-B bulbs, and well filtered. Another enclosure containing a 270-gallon preformed pond sunk to its rim in the ground is in a sunlit area of the backyard. It contains cold-tolerant fish and some Big Bend sliders.

The turtles and the fish coexist well, but despite the plants being of relatively distasteful varieties, the baby turtles sometimes graze on them extensively. Replacement plants are built into our maintenance plan and budget.

Maintaining water quality is important, but we are not fanatic about it. Being pond dwellers—turtles of quiet, sediment-filled waters, often with a rampant growth of aquatic and emergent vegetation—the sliders, the red-bellied cooters, and the painted turtles are a little more tolerant of varying water conditions than the river cooters and map turtles. Although we do not allow the aquaria to get even marginally dirty, we do full water changes a little less frequently than

we do in the tanks that hold river-dwelling turtles. Because the map turtles and the river cooters are more subject to bacterial shell problems than the red-ears and yellow-bellies, we also clean their power-head-activated sponge filters more frequently (perhaps twice a week).

Unfortunately, we cannot provide a precise formula for tank maintenance. How often maintenance is needed will depend on the number, size, and species of turtle you are keeping, the size of your tank, the diet being fed to the turtles, and the water quality that you begin with.

Our 250-gallon aquarium is home to about eight fast-growing riverine species (map turtles and others), all now having shell lengths of about 4 inches (10 cm). We start out with water that is about pH neutral.

We feed a diet heavy in earthworms and insects, keep edible vegetation always available, and change the water completely about every two weeks. Between changes, we clean the sponge filters two or three times and may do one partial water change.

On the other hand, the 150-gallon tank that contains the sliders receives filter maintenance about once every two weeks, gets no partial water changes, and gets a complete water change via flushing (we remove water and refill at the same time) only once every four to five weeks. Although the sliders also eat some worms and insects, a great proportion of their diet consists of turnip greens, chopped collard greens, elodea (an aquatic plant), and romaine lettuce.

The complete water flushing includes stirring the gravel, rinsing it, and treating the new water with a chlorine/chloramine remover. The turtles are put back when the tank temperature has risen to 78–85°F (26–29°C).

Garden Pools, Atriums, and Greenhouses

The adults of many of these turtles are so large that they are far more easily housed in an outside pool than in an inside tank. The pool may be outside (in northern climes this will undoubtedly restrict its usability during the months of winter) or it may be contained in an atrium or greenhouse. In normally warm areas, such as the southern tier states, outside pools may well be usable year-round, at least for turtles from temperate regions.

Pools can be as simple or as intricate as your imagination and budget allow.

Certainly the simplest and most inexpensive arrangement involves using either an aboveground or an in-ground kiddie wading pool. These are available during the spring and summer months at nearly every home supply store in the United States and in other areas of the world as well.

If used above ground, this pool will probably suffice only for seasonal use by large turtles or for baby turtles. In either case it will have to be covered. This will prevent larger specimens from escaping and smaller ones from being preyd upon by predatory birds or mammals, including family pets. Be sure that if you intend to use one of these, you purchase one without formed plastic ramps leading to the rim.

Position logs and/or smooth rocks in the center of the pond to create basking positions for the turtles. Fill the pool with your garden hose. To clean the water, you can simply run the water into the pool and let it overflow onto the surrounding ground. You can probably already see

The Cumberland slider lacks red ear markings and is seldom seen in captivity.

A portrait of a pastel yellow-bellied slider.

how this will be less work than an indoor enclosure. Keep the water level high enough so the turtles can totally submerge themselves. Do not over-crowd, and feed and clean as needed. You can hose off the algae or wipe down the pond as part of the cleaning process; don't add any sort of chemicals to kill or inhibit the algae. These might also be detrimental to the health of your turtles. The only problem with this type of pond is that it provides no land area for the female to lay her eggs, and eggs laid into water will literally drown.

Kiddie pools, sunk to their rim in the ground, can also be enclosed within a turtle-proof fence. This makes them much more usable, and helps stabilize water temperature as well. Pools either with or without a pre-formed ramp can be used in this setup, but one way or another, an exit ramp from the pool to the surrounding land area should be provided. This will enable your turtles to wander about at will upon the dry land, and should a female be carrying eggs, she can easily dig a hole to bury them. The height of the fence can be tailored to prevent the escape of the turtles housed here, but generally a 12-inch (30-cm) height with an overhang is sufficient.

These pools are seldom considered permanent enough to landscape with plants and gravel, but the area within the retaining fence can certainly be prettily planted with robust, nontoxic plants. Again, if necessary, use a fence overhang or a full cover when necessary to prevent the escape of, or predation on, the turtles.

In areas where temperatures get very hot (such as in our southwestern deserts) some method of keeping pool water acceptably cool (78–90°F [26–32°C]) yet allowing the turtles to avail themselves of the sun will need to be devised.

Perhaps placing the pond in a partially shaded area will alleviate at least part of the problem. Sinking the pond into the ground will also help,

This adult albino common red-ear (owned by Clive Longden) has an extraordinary amount of red on its face.

as will erecting a shade-cloth cover.

Once the location most suitable for the pond is determined, the actual setup—the digging, the fencing, and the landscaping—can begin.

Garden Pools

As we mentioned, garden pools can be as simple or as extravagant as you choose to make them. Besides the absolute simplicity and inexpensiveness offered by the kiddie wading pool, relatively nice-looking preformed pools varying from 20 gallons to 270 gallons in size can be purchased at garden centers and home-improvement stores. There is also the option of plastic linings or concrete.

A free-form pool that we constructed while in central Florida was about 20 feet long and a dozen feet wide. We even built a little bridge over the pool and would sit for long periods observing the many turtles it contained. Its depth varied from about 18 inches (45 cm) at the deepest point to about 12 inches (30 cm) at the shallow end. The pool was made of reinforced concrete, troweled to a smooth finish to ensure that the turtles did not abrade their plastrons while entering or leaving the water. This was home to about fifty turtles of fifteen species, ranging from cryptic matamatas to baskers such as common red-eared sliders and Barbour's map turtles.

We had far less elaborate pools while we were in southwest Florida. They were merely 8 foot diameter, galvanized cattle watering tanks. In these we maintained a water depth of about 18 inches (45 cm) and centered some large pieces of driftwood and sunken logs for haulout perches. In the pool that housed the (basically) nonherbivorous map turtles, we were even able to grow hardy water lilies as well as some potted emergent vegetation, thus enjoying both the activities of the turtles and the beauty of the plants.

The vegetation in the pool con-

Riverine species inhabit spring runs such as these. This is the home of the Rio Grande river cooter.

taining the sliders had to be tougher. The herbivorous preferences of these turtles restricted the growing plants to emergents such as Saint-John's-wort, cattails, and other nonpalatable species.

Atriums and Greenhouses

Atriums are now incorporated into many newer houses. They may be either open to the elements at the top, as in southern homes, or glass-covered. For our purposes, the comments made here about greenhouses apply equally to atriums.

Greenhouses of many styles, constructed from several types of materials, are readily available today. They are becoming ever more popular and are increasingly used by both hobbyists and commercial reptile and amphibian breeders. If properly heated and/or cooled, greenhouses can be ideal year-round homes for many aquatic turtles at any latitude.

This adult southern painted turtle is basking placidly.

What could be better for a dedicated hobbyist than having an enclosure not only ideal for your turtles, but in which, after it is thoughtfully set up, you can actually immerse (and lose) yourself as well? It is necessary to know that in many areas, greenhouses are considered permanent structures and a building permit is required to legally install one.

Building a greenhouse, and setting it up as a turtle home, can be a satisfying project. When installing or outfitting a greenhouse, you cannot give too much attention to detail. Security is essential, and heating (and cooling units, if the latter are needed) must be fully reliable. Securing a greenhouse against the escape of turtles is much easier than for any other type of reptile or amphibian. Double-entry doors, needed for the containment of many herp types, are not required.

In all cases, double glazing should be considered as an energy saving option, especially in regions subject to extreme cold or heat. We further suggest that the base of the unit either be flush against a concrete slab, affixed to a concrete or brick wall, or sunk a foot or more below the surface of the ground. This will preclude easy access by outside predators and escape by the turtles for which it has been designed. Remember that in the confines of a greenhouse, creatures such as white-footed and deer mice that are normally considered innocuous can actually become active predators or may chew and destroy cherished plantings. Normally predatory species such as weasels and shrews can wreak destruction overnight. The solution

Your Aquatic Turtles and the Role of Full-Spectrum Lighting

There seems to be a complex interaction in heliothermic reptiles (diurnal baskers) between the assimilation of ultraviolet rays (specifically UV-B), the natural synthesizing of vitamin D3, and the metabolism of calcium. To accommodate their need to bask and allow the best possible natural metabolizing of calcium, we provide a full-spectrum (UV-A and UV-B producing), high-intensity, basking light during the daylight hours. We use 100-watt, combined incandescent/fluorescent bulbs, 12 inches above the basking site. The light illuminates the exposed driftwood projections. Immediately below the lamp, the driftwood temperature is about 105°F (41°C). The turtles initially clamber to this area, but as they dry and warm sufficiently, they move to peripheral areas with somewhat lower temperatures. Although, if undisturbed, the baby turtles bask for long periods, they are perpetually ready to dive if startled.

Adults of all except the southern painted turtles and the comparatively diminutive male map turtles are so large that they are poorly suited for indoor aquaria. It is possible to keep large sliders and cooters inside, but even with large aquaria and excellent filtration, frequent water changes would be necessary. Adult aquatic turtles are best kept in garden pools, at least while seasonal temperatures allow. As would be expected, turtles from the more temperate areas of the USA (painted turtles and northern red-bellied turtles, for example) are quite cold tolerant, southern species and races are far less so, and those from the tropics must be protected from temperatures lower than 70°F (201°C). If their quarters are protected from freezing, the more northerly forms can be kept out year-round in the southern tier states. Southern and tropical turtles should be brought into an indoors aquarium during periods of cold weather.

lies in absolute prevention of visitation by predatory species—not in eradicating predators once they have gained access to your greenhouse.

For your turtles, either a temperate or tropical theme is equally effective. The design and building of your pond (and waterfall, if wanted) should be well thought out at the outset. It is often much easier to build your green-

house around the pond than to build the pond within the confines of an already erected greenhouse.

When constructed and landscaped with imagination, the interior of even a small greenhouse can be not only a safe haven for your cherished herps, but your own refuge from the vagaries of climate.

Feeding

Feeding Sliders and Cooters

The diet offered subadults and adults of the various sliders and cooters should be heavy on vegetation. The babies of these beautiful turtles tend to prefer a greater percentage of low-fat animal protein than the adults as their dietary staples. Pond plants such as elodea, cabomba, and the various eel grasses are favored dietary items. Additionally, romaine lettuce leaves, escarole, and mustard, dandelion, and collard greens can be given to these turtles. Trout chow, catfish chow, and koi pellets are also eaten, and are especially favored by the babies. Reptomin and commercial turtle chows may be offered as treats, or as a principal diet. Freshly killed (not thawed frozen) minnows, earthworms, crickets, and other insects are appreciated treats. When fish are frozen, the thiamine content is compromised. Therefore, if you do use thawed fish as a dietary item for your turtles, a thiamine additive should be provided.

The fresh vegetation and/or aquatic plants should always be available for turtles of all sizes, but the pelleted foods, insects, and fish should be fed only once every two or three days to subadult and adult turtles, and sparingly, but daily, to baby turtles. The animal-protein based foods should be fed only in amounts consumed within a few minutes of foraging. Uneaten animal protein foods can quickly foul your turtle's water. Feed amply, but prudently.

We have mentioned elsewhere the importance of proper calcium metabolizing by turtles, but this is so important that we would like to reiterate. In nature, the ultraviolet wavelength UV-B permits a reptile to synthesize vitamin D3. The presence of vitamin D3 allows calcium to be metabolized. Unless natural sunlight or the light from a very high-quality full-spectrum bulb is provided, both D3 and calcium dietary additives will be needed. But an overabundance of D3 can allow too much calcium to be metabolized, resulting eventually in visceral and articular gout. Fast-growing baby turtles and ovulating females require more calcium than adult males or nonovulating adult females. Unfortunately, there is no hard and fast formula for providing these additives, but we suggest that they be given once or twice weekly to baby turtles throughout the year and to females in the spring and early summer. At other times, provide the supplements once every two weeks to nonovulating females and adult males.

Liquid multivitamins (we use Avitron) and calcium additives are occasionally injected into the fish and worms. When this is done, and when other fatty foods are given, we move the turtles into a small and easily cleaned "feeding tank." Regularly feeding the turtles in a separate tank will help keep the main tank clean and will noticeably increase the duration between needed water changes.

The two central scutes of this eastern painted turtle are about to be shed.

Feeding Painted Turtles and Map Turtles

The turtles in these two genera are more carnivorous throughout their lives than the sliders and cooters. The preferred diet of a wild painted turtle or map turtle is heavy on aquatic insects, small crayfish, tadpoles, minnows—perhaps some carrion—and various non-noxious pond plants. Adult females of the broad-headed map turtles feed extensively on molluscs, a diet that can be difficult to supply to captives.

Captives eat such natural foods as earthworms, crickets, freshly killed minnows, and tadpoles. Small, softer-shelled snails, such as the pond snail and ramshorn snail, are eagerly devoured by all map turtles and help prevent overgrowth of horny edges of their mandibles. Prepared foods such as pelleted trout chow, catfish chow, and koi pellets are

eaten. Reptomin and scientifically formulated turtle chows are fine. Some vegetation should be offered. Pond plants and romaine lettuce leaves should be offered, but may not be eagerly consumed, especially by the map turtles. Remember that uneaten animal protein-based dietary items can quickly sour your water. Bacterial-laden water can quickly lead to shell rot in map turtles. Feed animal protein-based diets prudently.

When turtles are eating well, they grow quickly. Most of these basking species regularly shed the clear, keratinous, protective plates of the shell. This is natural, necessary, and not a cause for concern.

The sharp beak of a turtle, such as this common red-eared slider, is followed inside by bony crushing plates.

Not all veterinarians are qualified to treat ailing reptiles, nor do all choose to do so. Find a qualified veterinarian *before* you need his/her services.

The following are some typical turtle ailments.

Puffy eyelids or closed eyes often are the result of insufficient Vitamin A.

Soft shell (Metabolic Bone Disease) may be caused by an inability to metabolize calcium or by insufficient dietary calcium. Alter the amount of D3 and calcium provided. The wavelength UV-B permits a reptile to synthesize vitamin D3. This in turn allows calcium to be metabolized. Unless natural sunlight or the light from a very good full-spectrum bulb is provided, both D3 and cal-

cium dietary additives will be needed. We suggest that additives be given once or twice weekly to baby turtles and females in the spring and early summer; otherwise provide the supplements once every two weeks.

Ulcerative shell disease is usually caused by poor water quality and an inability to bask and dry properly. Improved hygiene is mandatory. Debridement, sensitivity tests, and medication may be required to correct an existing condition. Provide heated and illuminated basking/drying areas.

The riverine turtles are more susceptible to shell diseases than the pond turtles, and as a group the map turtles are very vulnerable. The problem is almost always associated with water

containing an untenably high bacterial count. Once started, there is virtually no way to curtail the problem before shell disfigurment has taken place, and even then the problem can be difficult to correct. Basking areas warmed and illuminated by UV-producing

This strangely marked, piebald common red-eared slider is in the collection of Clive Longden.

This is a pastel Florida red-bellied slider.

The white of this albino false map turtle is largely hidden by a patina of algae. (Clive Longden collection.)

This is a normally colored hatchling yellow-bellied slider.

bulbs, where these turtles can dry thoroughly, will help eliminate shell rot.

It is obvious that prevention rather than curing is the answer. The aquarium water in which captive map turtles swim must be kept scrupulously clean and relatively bacteria free. To accomplish this means strong filtration and frequent partial water changes. Consult a veterinarian if shell lesions are found.

Respiratory ailments can be caused by rapidly fluctuating or incorrect temperatures. Temporarily increase, and ultimately correct, the cage temperature regime. Medication may be necessary to cure these potentially fatal afflictions.

Dystocia (egg binding) can be caused by poorly formed eggs, but is most often caused by the female voluntarily retaining the eggs because of incorrect nesting conditions. Correct the nesting conditions (this usually means providing more, or less, moisture in the nesting area, or removing rocks or roots that may impede nesting). Oxytocin or another laying stimulant may be needed to induce laying. Consult a veterinarian.

Breeding

Breeding many of the sliders, cooters, painted turtles, and map turtles in captivity has now become rather commonplace. Yet, even though it is no longer a rarity, the successful hatching of a clutch of healthy baby turtles is one of the most exciting aspects of herpetoculture.

Most basking turtles, including the sliders, cooters, painted turtles, and map turtles, court and mate in the water. However, the eggs must be laid on land (eggs laid in the water will soon die). Females generally choose a barely moist, fairly sandy soil in which to nest. Once the female digs the nest, using her hind feet, she deposits the eggs and refills the nesting cavity. After this the female turtle tamps the surface with her feet and shell helping to obliterate traces of the nest. Most of this is accomplished with the female never actually turning around to see the nest or eggs.

Sexual maturity is attained by most female sliders, cooters, and the larger map turtles at a shell length of 6 to 8 inches (15–20 cm) and age of two to four years. Females of the painted turtles and smaller map turtles may lay eggs when only about 4 inches (10 cm) in length and two years of age.

Sexually mature males of some species (such as common red-eared sliders, western painted turtles, and false map turtles) develop greatly elongated foreclaws that are used to "tickle" the face and neck of the female during courtship. Sexually mature males also develop a long, thickened tail.

During courtship, males of the long-clawed types swim above and in front of the female (facing her), their foreclaws trembling in front of and against her face. The males of the short-clawed varieties merely trail a receptive female through the water, sometimes nipping at her face, neck, and legs, and at other times forgoing overt "courtship," simply mounting and breeding her. Juxtaposition of the cloacae and copulation occurs while the male holds the carapace of the female with his feet. Once bred, sperm retention by the female is possible. The female may actually produce fertile eggs for up to four years from a single breeding. Typically, a female will nest several times each season, digging a new nest for each clutch. The nest may be shallow or 4 or 5 inches (10–12 cm) deep. Females of some species (such as Suwannee cooters) may dig dummy nests, or nests with several chambers, perhaps as an antipredator mechanism. Healthy females of most species and subspecies (especially well-fed captives)

Beautiful and intricately marked, the Rio Grande river cooter is captive-bred by only a few hobbyists.

may nest from two to six times at about three-week intervals. There seems to be a tendency for older females to lay larger and fewer eggs. Females choose a sandy soil just on the moist side of dry for the nesting chamber. More than one nest may be started before the female determines that a site is suitable and deposition actually occurs. Nest construction and egg deposition may take from one to several hours. Eggs number from two to more than twenty, varying by species as well as the size of the female. Female sliders, cooters, and painted turtles seem to be less wary than most of the map turtles. Even wild examples of the former three species may nest in a relatively busy, heavily populated area (such as a backyard, or at the edge of a well-trodden trail). Nest construction and laying is often completed despite human traffic near the site. Female map turtles, on the other hand, are very wary. Nests may be constructed on sloping river or lake banks, but are often located on sandy, projecting sandbars. In keeping with their shy and wary demeanor, if disturbed, females searching for a nesting spot will usually run as quickly as possible back to the safety of the water. They are somewhat more approachable after egg deposition has actually begun.

The eggs of the turtles in these four genera are elongate and have a pliable shell. At 84°F (29°C) incubation is about fifty-eight to sixty-five days. Where temperatures are equable and predators (moles, raccoons, dogs, fire ants) are not a problem, and the nesting has occurred outside, the eggs can be left to incubate naturally. If you choose to incubate them inside, a chicken-egg incubator can be purchased (make sure you can lower the temperature to 82–85°F—some of the newer solid-state units are preset at higher temperatures for hen's eggs and not adjustable) from most livestock feed stores. The eggs can be half buried in a bed of barely moistened vermiculite, perlite, or sphagnum moss. It is best if the eggs are not turned on their long axis when removed from the nest or during incubation (see page 39).

Infertile or dead eggs may discolor or collapse. Shell collapse may also occur if the moisture content of the incubation substrate is insufficient. If the eggs smell bad, discard them. If not, continue incubation. Surprisingly bad-looking eggs can occasionally produce healthy hatchlings.

The sex of most (if not all) of these turtles is determined by nest temperature rather than genetically. This is termed TDSD—temperature-dependent sex determination. At cool temperatures females are produced; at hot temperatures, males are produced. At equable temperatures both sexes are produced. An ideal, and seemingly equable, incubation temperature for the eggs of most of these turtles is 83–85°F (28–29°C).

Attaining the correct moisture content and humidity for successful artificial incubation of eggs may take one or two tries. Nobody likes to fail, but because a female turtle usually lays several times each summer, a single failure does not mean failure for the year. Seek the help of an experienced herpetoculturist if you are in doubt.

The hatchlings of these turtles are truly endearing creatures. Varying by species, they are from 1 to 1.25 inches (2.5–3 cm) in length at emergence. Most hatchlings have vibrant colors, and those of the map turtles have saw-toothed posterior marginals and a very strong vertebral keel.

Hibernation, Photoperiod, Incubators, and Nesting

If you are merely keeping your turtles as pets, it is not necessary to consider hibernating them. Nor is it necessary to hibernate subtropical and tropical species and subspecies or to be concerned about photoperiod (day length versus night length). However, it appears that some turtles from northerly latitudes may require hibernation and a period of darkness, or at least a degree of cooling (for two to three months) and a reduced light cycle, to cycle reproductively. Simply cooling your turtles a little is usually an easy task. Whether they are kept indoors or out, Mother Nature will

This is a very pale (hypomelanistic) Mississippi map turtle.

In the case of the brightly colored western painted turtle, albinism detracts from its natural beauty. (Clive Longden collection.)

Making Your Own Incubator

Materials needed for one incubator:
1 wafer thermostat (obtainable from feed stores)
1 thermometer
1 Styrofoam cooler with thick sides (a fish shipping box is ideal)
1 heat tape or hanging heating coil (this will have an electrical cord and wall plug attached)
3 wire nuts
1 heavy wire shelf to hold egg containers 1 or 2 inches above the coiled heat tape

Your goal is to wire the thermostat into the circuitry between the heat-emitting tape and the electrical cord. This will allow you to set and maintain the proper incubation temperature for all manner of reptile eggs.

1. Cut the electrical cord about in half, but never leave less than 18 inches (45 cm) attached to the heat tape.
2. Poke a hole through the side of the cooler and pull the electrical cord through (keeping the plug on the outside). Do not plug this in until all modifications are complete.
3. Remove a half inch of insulation from both cut ends of the electrical cord and separate the two adjoined wires of each end for about 3 inches.
4. Carefully following the directions that come with the wafer thermostat, and using a wire nut, connect one of the exposed wire leads from the heat tape to the designated red wire of the thermostat. Use a second wire nut to connect the second of the thermostat's red wires to the plug in section of the electrical cord. With the third wire nut connect the remaining two bared wires (the unattached lead from the plug-in section to the still unattached lead from the heat tape).
5. Poke a small hole through the lid of the box and suspend the thermostat/heater from the inside.
6. You may poke another hole for a thermometer, so you can check on the inside temperature without opening the top. If there's no flange on the thermometer to keep it from slipping through the hole in the lid, use a rubber band wound several times around the thermometer to form a flange.
7. Put the lid on the cooler, and plug in the thermostat/heater. Wait half an hour and check the temperature. Adjust the thermostat/ heater until the temperature inside the incubator varies between 79 and 84°F (26–29°C). The L-pin "handle" on the top of the thermostat is the rheostat.
8. Once you have the temperature regulated, put the egg container shelf in place, place the container of eggs on the shelf inside the incubator, and close the lid.
   The incubator is now complete.

Slider, cooter, or pig-nosed turtle—all species of turtles lay eggs. This is a hatching Peninsula cooter.

A baby southern painted turtle greets the world. Photo by James Harding.

usually reduce temperatures (especially nighttime temperatures) by a few degrees during the winter months. If outdoors, natural photoperiods will prevail. This is often enough to stimulate breeding responses at the advent of the warmer temperatures and the longer days of spring.

However, hibernating a basking turtle can be a little more difficult. Your turtle's gut must be empty of food before the animal is hibernated. To be certain its gut is clear, stop feeding it about ten days prior to hibernation. Continue to provide water throughout the prehibernation fast. During hibernation you will be striving to reduce around-the-clock temperatures to 45–55°F (7–13°C). At these temperatures your turtle's metabolism will be slowed sufficiently so that it doesn't draw unduly on energy reserves during dormancy.

Letting an aquatic turtle hibernate naturally underwater in a small pond may work well in the southern tier states, including northern Florida. But to do so at northern latitudes is to invite disaster. In the north, it is better

to remove the turtles from their pond and hibernate them artificially. This can be done in a cool, dark basement, a root cellar, or even in a converted refrigerator. After you are certain the turtle's gut is free of digesting food, put the turtle in a box of slightly moist dead leaves or straw (its hibernaculum), and place the box in the cool, dark, designated area.

At the end of the hibernation period, move the box to a warmer, well-illuminated area and allow your turtle to become active. Once fully awakened, the turtle can be placed back in its pond.

Whether tropical or temperate in origin, if warm temperatures are provided, captive basking turtles will remain active year-round. Their

A hatchling northern red-bellied slider takes a breath.

The Suwannee cooter is a questionably distinct subspecies of the river cooter.

appetite may diminish somewhat and they may be a little more lethargic during the winter months. Although this is not natural for northern turtles, we have seen no indications of ill effects.

Basking turtle eggs are elongate and have a pliable shell. If given the opportunity, most females will dig a nesting chamber from one to several inches deep in which to lay their eggs. Should they happen to scatter the eggs in the terrarium, remove them carefully (keeping the same side up) from the terrarium and place them, half buried in the chosen, barely moistened, incubation substrate, in the incubator.

Check the temperature daily and add a little water to the incubating medium as needed. The preferred humidity is 80–90 percent. A saturated atmosphere, in which the moisture condenses and drips onto the eggs, is not wanted. The medium of vermiculite or perlite should be damp to the touch but too dry for you to squeeze out any water. Do not wet the eggs when you are remoistening the medium.

Infertile eggs may discolor and collapse. If you are certain the eggs are infertile, they may be removed and discarded. Embryo death may occasionally occur during incubation or, rarely, even as the full-term young are trying to break from their eggs.

At the end of the incubation period—which may vary (by species and incubation temperature) from about sixty-five to more than ninety days—hatching will occur.

Assisted by some biodegradation of the shell, the hatchlings cut their way free of the egg with an "egg

The intricate belly pattern of this hatchling Ouachita map turtle will soon become indistinct.

tooth" or caruncle (this tooth drops off in a few days). It may take a day or longer for the hatchlings to finally emerge from the eggs. When they emerge from their eggs, hatchling chelonians usually have large umbilical egg sacs. These are absorbed sometime in the next few hours to two days. The hatchlings will not need, or even want, to feed until the egg sac has been fully used.

Hatchling sliders, cooters, painted turtles, and map turtles are much more delicate than the adults. To prevent them rupturing the exposed yolk sac, keep the hatchling on dampened paper towels until the yolk sac has been absorbed.

The hatchlings should be moved to a small terrarium and offered food, a sunning spot, an area of seclusion (damp sphagnum moss in which they can burrow is ideal), and water.

Provide all hatchlings with an even warmth for the first few weeks of their life.

If you take the hatchlings outside, remember that predators come in many forms. Jays, crows, and grackles all eagerly eat baby turtles. Fire (and other) ants can quickly find hatchlings on the ground. Cats, dogs, opossums, mice, rats, and raccoons are all dangerous to your babies. Sunlight

itself, usually a coveted ally in the breeding and raising of turtles, can become an adversary and quickly overheat an improperly situated container.

To successfully breed basking turtles, you must provide a suitable nesting area. Those that are well acclimated to captivity will most often nest as naturally as they would in the wild. Most females dig a well-defined nest that is just about as deep as the turtles are able to reach with their hind feet. These turtles prefer soil that is just damp enough to retain its integrity as the nesting chamber is dug. Collapsing sides or insufficient depth of nesting medium may compel the female to temporarily discontinue her nesting attempts and restart elsewhere.

As she digs her nest, the female turtle moistens the soil with water from her bladder. As the eggs are laid, the female reaches down into the nest with a hind foot and positions each one. The descent of the dropping eggs may be slowed somewhat by the expulsion of a thick, viscous fluid from the female's vent. Once the laying is completed, the female covers the nest and methodically tamps down the covering dirt.

Depending on the time of year, the rainfall, and the species of turtle that laid them, after the female has laid and covered her clutch, you may prefer to remove and artificially incubate them rather than leave them in place. Carefully place the eggs in the position in which they laid in the nest in small plastic containers half filled with dampened vermiculite. Put these cups into the incubator.

It is not unusual to find Ouachita map turtles with algae covering their shell.

Many adult males of sliders and related turtles develop long foreclaws as a secondary sexual characteristic. This is a male Florida red-bellied cooter.

Many herpetoculturists think it is very important not to rotate the eggs on either longitudinal axis when they are removed. Although we do not think this is absolutely essential, neither do we tempt fate. To help us with egg orientation, we pencil a small X on the top of each egg before it is moved. Once laid, turtle eggs, unlike bird eggs, do not require turning during incubation, and at some points in the incubation, turning the egg may be fatal to the developing embryo.

If you allow the eggs of your turtles to incubate naturally, be certain that they are protected from predators.

Many birds will watch a nesting female and steal the eggs as they are laid. These birds and mammalian predators will also dig the eggs from the nests and eat them, or eat newly hatched babies.

These Rio Grande cooters are recently hatched.

The Ouchita map turtle is beautiful and alert.

Breeding turtles and watching your very own captive-bred and hatched young grow and mature can be immensely satisfying, but it is also a lengthy endeavor that requires much thought and care.

Obtaining Aquatic Turtles

Today, many of our more commonly seen baby turtles remain quite inexpensive and readily available. It is seldom necessary to go farther than the neighborhood pet store to find such common types as red-ears, yellow-bellies, and Mississippi map turtles. However, finding some of the more uncommon forms, including some of the increasingly popular tropical species, subspecies, as well as designer color morphs, may take a more diligent search. For these it will be necessary to check specialty breeders and dealers (many list in the classified sections of reptile magazines), vendors at herp expos, or Web/advertisements.

It is always exciting to find the particular form for which you are searching, but once you have found

it in some region of the country distant from you, what happens next?

Often, things are rather straightforward from that point on.

You find, you buy, the turtle is shipped to you, the deal is done, and you and the seller (and ideally the baby turtle) are all happy. But let's explore this transaction a little more closely and look at turtle sources as well.

Whether your purchase is from a classified ad, the Web, or at an expo, we urge you to research the integrity of your vendor before any transaction. The good part of the Internet is that it makes selling, purchasing, and by asking fellow hobbyists, ascertaining the honesty of the dealer easy. The bad part about the net is that anyone—including unscrupulous sellers—can easily advertise, so use care. This holds true of ads in other media as well, and at some of the less-regulated herp expos. Stated simply, if you know both the product you seek and the vendor who sells it, the chances are pretty good that the transaction will be satisfactory.

Because you deal one on one with the sellers, reptile swap meets (or

This Mississippi map turtle has a more strongly marked head than most.

Midland painted turtles bask on a sunny snag in a Michigan lake.

"expos") are a little safer than the Web for plying uncharted waters. These shows are often excellent sources of specimens. Get-togethers of breeders and potential purchasers are held in many of the larger cities across the United States and Europe. The shows may vary in size from only a dozen or so vendors to some that host upward of 400 vendors. One of the largest of these, a weekend event held annually in a gigantic convention center in central Florida, has 500 vendor tables and more than 10,000 attendees.

Shipping

Let's take a quick look at the whys and wherefores of purchasing a turtle on the Web.

Unless you are known to your seller, chances are good that they will insist on prepayment. It is because of this that we again stress the importance of thoroughly checking the integrity of the seller.

Barring prepayment, some shippers may suggest that the shipment be made COD. Although entirely possible, and actually a viable alternative to prepayment, "hidden" charges, invariably make COD more expensive, and often more inconvenient, than prepaying.

Turtles can not be legally shipped via the U.S. Postal Service, but such door-to-door carriers as UPS, FedEx, and Airborne may handle them. Call to determine if "perishable" shipments are allowed. The cost for door-to-door service is in the $20–$30 range. Although these carriers will require that someone be home to sign the waybill when delivery is made, this is a relatively convenient method of shipment that is actually cheaper—or at least no more expensive—than the airport-to-airport alternative.

Whichever you choose, in most cases you will pay for both the animal and the shipping charges in advance. Your shipper will need your credit card number and expiration date, a money order, or a cashier's check. Many shippers will accept personal checks but wait until the check clears the bank before shipping (usually within a week or so).

Once a method of payment is hashed out, the supplier will need your full name, physical address (a P.O. box or rural route number will not suffice) and day and night telephone numbers. If you have opted for

Two red ear markings typify common red-eared sliders from southern Texas.

airport-to-airport service, be certain that your shipper knows exactly which destination airport to use. Agree on a shipping date, and on that date call your supplier for the waybill number. Some shippers go to the airport on one or two specific days each week, but may ship more frequently on the door-to-door carriers. Avoid weekend shipments. Some carriers may provide shipment status tracing on their web site.

Most shipments take about twenty-four hours to get from the shipper to the purchaser. Shipping may become difficult (and should be avoided) during very hot weather, very cold weather, or during the peak holiday travel/shipping/mailing times.

Once it has arrived, claim and inspect your shipment as quickly as possible. This is especially important in bad weather. If you have opted for airport-to-airport service, learn the hours of your cargo office and whether the shipment can be picked up at the ticket counter if it arrives after the cargo office has closed. If you use COD, you will need to pay all charges in full before you are allowed to inspect your shipment. Open and inspect your shipment before leaving the cargo facility. Unless otherwise specified, reliable shippers guarantee live delivery. However, if there is a problem, both the shipper and the airline(s), will require that a "carrier's discrepancy" or "damage" report be made out, signed, and dated by carrier personnel. In the very rare case when a problem has occurred, insist on filling out and filing a claim form right then and contact your shipper immediately for instructions.

Although this may sound complicated, you will probably find that the transportation by air of a wanted turtle is easy, fast, and safe. However, it is not always inexpensive. Be sure to compare the charges assessed by all carriers.

A southern slider basks atop floating plants.

Glossary

Aestivation: A period of warm weather inactivity; often triggered by excessive heat or drought.

Albino: Lacking black pigment.

Ambient temperature: The temperature of the surrounding environment.

Anterior: Toward the front.

Articular: Pertaining to the joints.

Anus: The external opening of the cloaca; the vent.

Bridge: The "bridge of shell" between fore and rear limbs that connects the carapace and the plastron.

Brumation: The reptilian and amphibian equivalent of mammalian hibernation.

Carapace: The upper shell of a chelonian.

cb/cb: Captive-bred, captive-born.

cb/ch: Captive-bred, captive-hatched.

Chelonian: A turtle or tortoise.

Cloaca: The common chamber into which digestive, urinary and reproductive systems empty and which itself opens exteriorly through the vent or anus.

Clutch: A single deposition of eggs.

Crepuscular: Active at dusk and/or dawn.

Deposition: As used here, the laying of the eggs or birthing of young.

Deposition site: The nesting site.

Dimorphic: A difference in form, build, or coloration involving the same species; often sex-linked.

Dorsal: Pertaining to the back; upper surface.

Dorsum: The upper surface.

Ectothermic: "Cold-blooded."

Endemic: Confined to a specific region.

Endothermic: "Warm-blooded."

Form: An identifiable species or subspecies.

Genus: A taxonomic classification of a group of species having similar characteristics. The genus falls between the next higher designation of "family" and the next lower designation of "species."

Genera: The plural of genus.

Glottis: The opening of the windpipe.

Gravid: The reptilian equivalent of mammalian pregnancy.

Heliothermic: Pertaining to a species that basks in the sun to thermoregulate.

Herbivorous: Plant-eating.

Herpetoculture: The captive breeding of reptiles and amphibians.

Herpetoculturist: One who practices herpetoculture.

Herpetologist: One who indulges in herpetology.

Herpetology: The study (often scientifically oriented) of reptiles and amphibians.

Hibernation: Winter dormancy.

Hybrid: Offspring resulting from the breeding of two species.

A portrait of a western painted turtle.

Intergrade: Offspring resulting from the breeding of two subspecies.

Juvenile: A young or immature specimen.

Keel: A carapacial or plastral ridge (or ridges).

Lateral: Pertaining to the side.

Mandibles: Jaws.

Mandibular: Pertaining to the jaws.

MBD: Metabolic Bone Disease caused by low calcium in diet.

Melanism: A profusion of black pigment.

Middorsal: Pertaining to the middle of the back.

Monotypic: Containing only one type.

Multi-clutch: Lay more than one set of eggs per year.

Nocturnal: Active at night.

Omnivorous: Eating plant and animal matter.

Ontogenetic: Age-related (color) changes.

Orbit: The eye socket.

Oviparous: Reproducing by means of eggs that hatch after laying.

Photoperiod: The daily/seasonally variable length of the hours of daylight.

Plastron: The bottom shell.

Poikilothermic (also ectothermic): A species with no internal body temperature regulation. The old term was "cold-blooded."

Postocular: To the rear of the eye.

Race: A subspecies.

Saxicolous: Rock-dwelling.

Scute: Scale.

Seams: The growing edges of the shell scutes.

Species: A group of similar creatures that produce viable young when breeding. The taxonomic designation that falls beneath genus and above subspecies. Abbreviation, "sp."

Subspecies: The subdivision of a species. A race that may differ slightly in color, size, scalation, or other criteria. Abbreviation, "ssp."

Sympatric: Occurring together.

Taxonomy: The science of classification of plants and animals.

Terrestrial: Land-dwelling.

Thermoregulate: To regulate (body) temperature by choosing a warmer or cooler environment.

Vent: The external opening of the cloaca; the anus.

Venter: The underside of a creature; the belly.

Ventral: Pertaining to the undersurface or belly.

Helpful Information

Herpetological Societies

Reptile and amphibian interest groups exist in the form of clubs, monthly magazines, and professional societies, in addition to the herp expos and other commercial functions mentioned elsewhere.

Herpetological societies (or clubs) exist in major cities in North America, Europe, and other areas of the world. Most have monthly meetings, some publish newsletters, and many host or sponsor field trips or picnics, or indulge in various other interactive functions. Among the members are enthusiasts of varying expertise. Information about these clubs can often be learned by querying pet shop employees, high school science teachers, university biology department professors, or curators or employees at the department of herpetology at local museums and zoos. All such clubs welcome inquiries and new members.

The following professional herpetological societies produce publications

Society for the Study of Amphibians
and Reptiles (SSAR)
Robert D. Aldrich, Treasurer
Department of Biology
St. Louis University
St. Louis, MO 63013

Herpetologists' League
Division of Biological Sciences
Emporia State University
Emporia, Kansas 66801

The SSAR publishes two quarterly journals: *Herpetological Review* contains husbandry, geographic range, news on ongoing field studies, and so on, and the *Journal of Herpetology* contains articles oriented more towards academic herpetology.

The Herpetologists' League publishes a quarterly bulletin and occasional monographs.

Reptiles magazine publishes articles on all aspects of herpetology and herpetoculture (including aquatic turtles). This monthly publication also carries classified ads and news about herp expos. Contact *Reptiles* at

Reptiles magazine
P.O. Box 6050
Mission Viejo, CA 92690

One of the most important Internet addresses is *www.kingsnake. com*. This site provides an immensely active classified section, interactive forums, periodic chats, and Web-radio interviews. Because of the ability to post and view photos of the many turtles being offered for sale, this site should be of great interest to all hobbyists.

Index

Page numbers set in boldface type indicate photographs.